FRANCIS FRITH'S

A Taste of
YORKSHIRE

REGIONAL RECIPES FROM YORKSHIRE

Illustrated with historical photographs from
The Francis Frith Collection

FRANCIS FRITH'S

A Taste of

YORKSHIRE

York, Goodramgate 1892 30631

Compiled by Julia Skinner

THE FRANCIS FRITH COLLECTION

First published in the United Kingdom by
The Francis Frith Collection exclusively for Identity Books in 2009
Paperback Edition ISBN 978-1-84589-422-1

British Library Cataloguing in Publication Data

A Taste of Yorkshire
Julia Skinner

The Francis Frith Collection®
Frith's Barn, Teffont,
Salisbury, Wiltshire SP3 5QP
Tel: +44 (0) 1722 716 376
Email: info@francisfrith.co.uk
www.francisfrith.com

Printed and bound in Malta

Front Cover: Knaresborough, Market Day 1921 71687t
The colour-tinting in this image is for illustrative purposes only, and is not intended
to be historically accurate.

CONTENTS

INTRODUCTION

Travel around Yorkshire through the pages of this book and discover a selection of the delicious traditional food of the area, as well as some of the stories and fascinating facts behind the recipes. Your journey will be given added savour by the historical images taken by photographers from The Francis Frith Collection, showing the people and places of Yorkshire in the past.

Regional traditional dishes were developed from the local produce that was available to thrifty housewives who had to feed large, hungry families on a limited budget. Many of the old recipes also reflect the limited cookery techniques that were available in the past, as well as the skills of the cooks who were able to provide cheap and tasty meals with only a fire, a skillet and a cauldron to cook with, often producing the historical version of 'boil in the bag' meals.

This book is not intended to provide a comprehensive collection of the local recipes of the region, and some recipes are modern interpretations using some of the fine local produce that the area is famous for, but we hope that the food described within these pages, as well as the descriptions of traditional customs, sayings and local dialect words, will provide you with a taste of Yorkshire.

Haworth, Top Withens, ' Wuthering Heights' 1958 H194045

Wetherby, North Street 1909 61731

Hull, Market Place 1903 49809

FISH

Yorkshire fishermen have ventured out for centuries from small villages such as Runswick Bay, larger harbours such as Bridlington and Whitby, and the great port and fishing centre of Hull. In its day, Hull was the great fishing port of the British Empire, and was once the home of the world's largest deep-water fishing fleet. Hull trawlers fished the North Sea, the White Sea, and the fringes of the Arctic, particularly for cod.

Bridlington, Men on the Quay c1885 18042x

RECIPE

North Sea Fisherman's Pie

In former years a fish pie was the traditional dish to be eaten at Easter, on Good Friday.

For the filling:
350ml/12 fl oz milk
1 bay leaf
Half an onion, finely sliced
450g/1 lb haddock or cod fillet
225g/8oz smoked haddock fillet
3 hard-boiled eggs, chopped
25g/1oz butter or margarine
25g/1oz plain flour
75g/3oz shelled prawns
2 tablespoonfuls chopped fresh parsley
Lemon juice to taste

For the topping:
500g /1¼ lbs potatoes, cooked
40g/1½ oz butter
60ml/ 4 tablespoonfuls milk
115g/4oz grated hard cheese of choice
Salt and pepper

Place the milk, the bay leaf and sliced onion in a saucepan over a medium heat and add the fish. Cover, and poach the fish lightly for 10 minutes. Strain, discard the bay leaf and reserve the milk for the sauce. Flake the fish into a buttered pie dish, discarding the skin and any remaining bones. Add the chopped eggs to the fish.

Melt 25g/1oz butter in a saucepan on a low heat, stir in the flour and cook gently for 1 minute, stirring continually. Remove the pan from the heat and stir in the reserved milk that the fish was poached in, a little at a time and stirring continually so that no lumps are formed. When all the milk has been mixed in, return the pan to the heat and bring the mixture to the boil, stirring continually as the sauce thickens, then simmer the sauce for about 4 minutes, still stirring all the time. Remove from the heat and stir in the prawns.

Add the parsley, lemon juice and seasoning to taste. Pour the sauce over the fish and eggs in the pie dish, and gently mix it all together.

Pre-heat the oven to 180°C/350°F/Gas Mark 4.

To make the topping

Gently heat 40g/1½ oz butter in 60ml/ 4 tablespoonfuls of milk in a small saucepan until the butter melts, then add the milk and melted butter to the cooked potatoes, mash and then beat until smooth. Spoon over the fish pie mixture to cover, then score the surface with a fork. Sprinkle the grated cheese over the pie before baking. Bake the pie in the pre-heated oven for 25-30 minutes, until the top is golden.

Local words and phrases from the Scarborough area

'Beck' - a stream.

'Ginnel' - an alleyway between houses.

'Gradely' - good, as in 'It were reet gradely' - It was really good.

'Growler' - pork pie.

'Keks' - trousers.

'Lake' or 'laik' - to play, or skive off work, as in 'Is he laiking again?'

'Allus at't last push up'- always at the last moment.

'Brass-necked' - very confident.

'If tha' dances wi' devil, thal' ge't pricked wi'-is 'orn' - If you dance with the devil you'll get pricked by his horns, ie you will suffer if you do evil deeds.

'Think on' - Think about it.

'It caps owt' - it beats everything.

Scarborough, The Pierhead
1890 23472

Staithes, Baiting the Lines c1900 S176001

At the attractive fishing village of Staithes, Whitby-built yawls and cobles ventured out in pairs to catch haddock, cod and mackerel. Each of the yawls had a ten-man crew, and the cobles that trailed them had three-man crews. When the yawls were sinking under the weight of the fish, the catch was transferred to the cobles. There were 300 vessels at Staithes in the 1850s. The larger vessels followed the shoals, and ventured as far south as Yarmouth each September to join the huge East Anglian herring fleets.

This photograph shows fish wives and old men at Staithes, baiting the lines. The women are wearing traditional bonnets, which were flared at the sides to stop the coils of hooks and lines becoming entangled in their hair. Each bonnet required a yard of material, and was double-plaited at the front and tied at the back with a bow. To this day some of the women of Staithes still wear these bonnets. White in colour, when a woman is widowed the colour of the material is then changed to black, which is worn for a considerable time after the bereavement. This bonnet, in turn, is exchanged for one of a mauve coloured material.

RECIPE

~ . ~

Buttered Crab

Shellfish, lobster and crab are found along the Yorkshire coast.

> 450g/1 lb fresh or frozen crab meat
> 2 anchovy fillets
> 150ml/5 fl oz dry white wine
> A pinch of grated nutmeg or mace
> 4 tablespoonfuls fresh white breadcrumbs
> Salt and freshly ground black pepper
> 75g/3oz butter

Flake the crab meat coarsely. Pound up the anchovies in the wine, and add the nutmeg, breadcrumbs and seasonings. Put into a saucepan and bring gently to the boil, then simmer for 3 minutes. Mix the flaked crab meat with the butter and add to the hot wine mixture, stir and cook gently for 4 minutes. Serve the buttered crab with slices or fingers of hot buttered toast.

~ . ~

Hull, St Andrew's Dock c1955   H133037

RECIPE

— · —

Cod, Lemon and Lime Fishcakes

This recipe is a reminder of Hull's deep-water fishing tradition.

> 750g/1½ lbs thick cod fillet
> 450g/1 lb large new potatoes, scrubbed and parboiled
> Half an onion, grated
> Zest of 1 lemon and 1 lime
> Juice of 1 lime
> Salt and freshly ground black pepper
> 2 tablespoonfuls sunflower oil

Place the cod fillet in a pan, and cover with water. Heat until the water simmers for 2 minutes, then turn off the heat, cover the pan and leave to cool. Alternatively the fish can be cooked in a microwave, covered with film, on a high setting for about 3 minutes, and then left to cool. When cooked and cooled, flake the fish into large pieces.

Grate the potatoes into a bowl, and add the flaked fish and grated onion, the lemon and lime zest and lime juice. Season with salt and freshly ground black pepper to taste. Shape the mixture with your hands on a floured surface into 8 thick fishcakes, place them on a plate and leave to rest in the fridge for 10 minutes.

Heat the oil in a frying pan and fry the fishcakes on one side until they are crusty and browned, then turn them and cook the other sides.

— · —

St Andrew's Dock in Hull (see opposite page) was originally intended for the use of the coal industry, but immediately after opening in 1883 it was named after the patron saint of fishermen and handed over for the exclusive use of Hull's 420 fishing smacks. An economic survey of the 1950s stated that there were probably around 50,000 people in Hull, or one fifth of the population, involved with the fishing industry. Sadly, St Andrew's Dock closed in 1975, and the site has now been redeveloped as the St Andrew's Quay leisure and retail complex; hardly any trace remains now of Hull's once great fishing industry.

RECITE

—·—

Herrings were a particularly important catch for north-eastern fishermen in the 19th century. Herrings, known to fishermen as the 'silver darlings', are particularly nutritious and were sought after as a staple part of the diet in Victorian times. A mustard sauce is a favourite accompaniment to herrings in many parts of north-east England.

Herrings in Oatmeal

4 herrings
50g/2oz medium oatmeal
Half a teaspoonful of salt
25-50g/1-2oz butter
Juice of half a lemon
Chopped fresh parsley

Clean and bone the herrings, and dry them. Mix the salt in with the oatmeal, and use this to coat the herrings on both sides, pressing the oatmeal well into the fish. Melt the butter in a frying pan and fry the herrings for about 3 minutes on each side, adding more butter as necessary. Place the cooked fish on a hot dish and keep warm.

Add a little more butter to the pan, and when it is melted and frothy add the lemon juice, pour over the fish and sprinkle with chopped parsley, or alternatively serve the fish with mustard sauce (recipe on opposite page).

—·—

RECIPE

Mustard Sauce

This mustard sauce can be used with chicken, ham, pork, bacon and sausages, but in the north-east of England it is often served as an accompaniment for fish, especially grilled or fried herring and mackerel. Mustard sauce was also a traditional accompaniment to the boar's head which was often served at Christmas.

> 25g/1oz butter
> 25g/1oz plain flour
> 1 teaspoonful of vinegar
> 1 teaspoonful of caster sugar
> Salt and pepper
> 1-2 teaspoonfuls mustard powder (according to taste)
> 300ml/½ pint milk

Melt the butter in a double saucepan. Stir in the flour, and add the milk a little at a time, stirring continuously. Bring to the boil, then simmer until the sauce thickens, still stirring. Remove from heat. Blend together the mustard powder, sugar and vinegar to a smooth cream and stir into the sauce, mixing well. Season to taste. Heat through just before serving, but do not let the sauce boil.

Whitby, 'Gemini' 1891
28862

These two children
are in fact boys, and
have been identified
as Matthew Peart
(left) and Robert Peart
(right). They were twin
brothers, as the original
title of the photograph
implies.

Whitby, Fish Quay 1923 74318

RECITE

— • —

Stuffed Mackerel with Gooseberry Sauce

Gooseberries have long been a traditional accompaniment to mackerel in English cookery. Cold smoked mackerel fillets are also delicious eaten with brown bread and butter and a portion of gooseberry jam as a relish.

4 mackerel, gutted and de-scaled
1 tablespoonful chopped parsley
1 tablespoonful chopped thyme
Half a teaspoonful grated lemon rind
1 tablespoonful lemon juice
25g/1oz soft white breadcrumbs
Seasoned flour
225g/8oz gooseberries
Sugar to taste
A little butter or oil

Wash and dry the mackerel and clean them. Mix the parsley, thyme, lemon rind, lemon juice and soft breadcrumbs and stuff the mackerel with this mixture. Roll the fish lightly in seasoned flour. Melt a little butter or oil in a baking pan and, when it is very hot, put in the mackerel. Put into the oven and bake at 180°C/350° F/Gas Mark 4 for 25 minutes, carefully turning the fish over halfway through.

Meanwhile, for the gooseberry sauce, simmer the gooseberries in a very little water until they are soft. Rub them through a sieve and sweeten lightly, with the sugar, to taste.

Warm the gooseberry sauce through before serving with the mackerel.

— • —

MEAT AND GAME

The moors and dales of Yorkshire are grazed by sheep, which for centuries provided the raw material for the county's important textile industry. However, sheep have also played a part in Yorkshire's food history – it was sheeps' milk which was first used by the monks of Jervaulx Abbey to produce Wensleydale cheese, and a special cut for a lamb chop is named after the Yorkshire town of Barnsley – a Barnsley chop is cut from the centre of the loin across both chops, producing a butterfly shape.

Malham, A Sheep Sale on the Green c1910 M139023

RECIPE

— · —

Savoury Lamb Pie

For the pie filling:
450g/1 lb of lean lamb, cut into small cubes
1 dessertspoonful of plain flour
Salt and pepper
1 medium sized onion, sliced
1 large cooking apple, peeled, cored and thinly sliced
150ml/ ¼ pint stock, preferably made from lamb bones

For the scone topping:
175g/6oz self-raising flour
¼ teaspoonful of salt
1 teaspoonful chopped mixed herbs
25g/1oz margarine
25g/1oz lard
125ml/3-4fl oz milk

Pre-heat the oven to 180°C/350°F/Gas Mark 4.

Add salt and pepper to the flour. Toss the cubes of meat in the seasoned flour to coat them on all sides. Place the meat in a shallow 2 pint casserole, and sprinkle on the remaining seasoned flour. Layer the sliced onions on top of the meat, then the sliced apple, and pour over the water or stock. Cover the casserole with the lid and bake in the pre-heated oven for 1½ to 2 hours, until the lamb is tender (the time depends on the quality of the lamb used).

Increase the oven heat to 220°C/425°F/Gas Mark 7, ready to add the scone topping.

To make the scone topping: place the self-raising flour in a bowl, and add the salt and herbs. Rub in the fats, then add as much of the milk as is needed to mix it all to a soft dough. Roll out the dough to about ½ cm (¼ inch) thick, and cut into rounds about 6cm (2½ inches) in diameter.

Take the casserole out of the oven. Arrange the scone rounds on top of the pie filling, and return the casserole to the oven without its lid. Bake for a further 25-30 minutes, until the scone top is golden and crusty.

— · —

Bradford, Darley Street 1897 39508

Meat and Potato Pie

The author J B Priestley provided Britain with a rather strange morale-boosting symbol from Yorkshire during the Second World War – a meat and potato pie.

The pie that inspired Priestley had been a feature in the window of Arthur Roberts's food shop in Godwin Street in Bradford for around 40 years; it actually consisted of a pie crust over an empty pie dish, which concealed a mechanism that puffed steam out of holes in the crust at intervals. During the war, Priestley was broadcasting a series of radio talks on Sunday evenings, and one day he visited Bradford just after the window of Arthur Roberts's shop had been blown off in an air raid. He happened to wander past the shop, and there, in the partly boarded-up window, was the pie, still puffing away and trying to entice shoppers to come in and buy. Priestley described the scene in his next radio broadcast:

'… a giant, almost superhuman meat pie, with a magnificent brown, crisp, artfully wrinkled, succulent-looking crust … giving off a fine, rich, appetising steam to make your mouth water … a perpetual volcano of meat and potato … every puff defying Hitler, Goering and the whole gang of them'.

It became one of Priestley's best-known broadcasts, much to the annoyance of Mr Roberts, who soon grew tired of crowds of people flocking to stand outside his shop and watch the famous, bravely defiant puffing pie.

Local words and phrases from the Bradford area

'Tyke' - the broad Yorkshire dialect.

'Put 't wood in 't 'oil!' - close the door!

'Shuck' - crazy.

'E's double fisted an' threpple thrioted' - someone who is both aggressive and a heavy drinker (double fisted and triple throated).

'A brussen tup' - someone who is full of his own importance.

'Ginnel' - an alley or narrow passageway.

'Ippens' - nappies.

'Featherlegged' - very tired.

'Sackless' - lazy.

'Muckment' - rubbish, refuse.

RECIPE

—·—

Meat and Potato Pie

450g/1 lb beef stewing steak
1 heaped tablespoonful of plain flour
Salt and pepper
A small amount of fat or oil for frying
1 onion, sliced
300ml/ ½ pint brown stock
225g/8oz potatoes
225g/8oz shortcrust or puff pastry

Cut the meat into cubes, trimming off any fat. Mix the salt and pepper into the flour, and toss the meat in the seasoned flour, to cover all sides. Melt the fat or oil in a saucepan and fry the sliced onion and the meat for a few minutes, turning the cubes of meat so that they are sealed and browned on all sides. Add the stock to the saucepan. Bring to the boil, then cover the pan with its lid, reduce the heat and simmer for about 1½ hours.

When the meat is tender, put the meat and gravy into a pie dish. Peel the potatoes and cut them into small cubes, then add them to the meat.

Pre-heat the oven to 220°C/425°F/Gas Mark 7.

Roll out the pastry on a floured board, to be slightly larger than the pie dish. Cut off a narrow strip from the pastry, and fit it around the dampened rim of the dish, then brush the pastry strip with water. Lay the pastry over the dish, and press the edges of the lid and the pastry strip together all around the rim to seal them. Make a small slit in the middle of the lid with a sharp knife to make a hole for the steam to escape, then brush the pastry lid with milk or beaten egg to glaze.

Bake in the pre-heated oven for 20 minutes, then lower the temperature to 180°C/350°F/Gas Mark 4 and bake for a further 20 minutes, until the pastry is golden and crisp.

—·—

Keighley, The Cattle Market c1910 K60504

The photograph on the opposite page shows the historic Shambles of the city of York. The word 'shambles' comes from the Old English 'shamel', which means a bench or a stall, and in medieval York this was the area where the butchers prepared and sold meat from such 'shambles'. The wide shelves for displaying meat can be seen at the front of the shops in this photograph, and these and the hooks overhead indicate that even in the early years of the 20th century this was still the traditional part of the city for butchers' shops. The narrowness of the street kept the shops cool in the days before refrigeration, and prevented direct sunlight from reaching the meat.

York, Children in the Shambles 1909 61722x

Aldborough, Children and Cart 1907 58636x

Local words and phrases from the York area

'Appen' - perhaps.

'Fendable' - capable.

'It fair trim'd ma' - that suited me perfectly, as of a present.

'Liggin' - lying down.

'Lop' - a flea.

'Menseful' - neat, orderly, decent. 'It will mense it off'- It will finish something off nicely.

'Putten aboot' - harrassed, very busy.

'Side the table' - clear the table.

'Stagnated' or 'fair capp'd' - greatly surprised.

'Stall'd' - fed up with, wearied or tired of something.

This photograph shows the statue of Richard Oastler in its original position in Forster Square in Bradford. Richard Oastler fought against the use of child labour in the industrial mills, including those in Bradford. The statue of 'The Factory King' was later considered a traffic nuisance and was moved to Rawson Square; in recent years it was moved again to its present site on North Parade.

Bradford's children had cause to be grateful to another man concerned for their welfare in the opening years of the 20th century. In 1904 Bradford City Council decided to provide free school meals for all local schoolchildren, a move initiated by Councillor Fred Jowett in response to the hunger and illness that the city's working-class schoolchildren were perceived to be suffering. By doing this, the city council was breaking the law of the time, which forbade such expenditure from local council funds. Bradford City Council argued that if the law made it compulsory for parents to send children to school, then the council had an obligation to feed them whilst they were there. In 1906 Fred Jowett was elected Bradford's Member of Parliament, and was responsible for the implementation of an Education Act which empowered local authorities nationally to provide free school meals for those children in need.

Bradford, Forster Square 1897 39506x

Guisborough, The Buck Hotel, Market Place
1907 58660x

RECIPE

— · —

Poor Man's Goose

Roast Goose was traditionally eaten at Michaelmas at the end of September, and was often served with a savoury suet pudding. In many parts of Yorkshire it was the custom to make Goose Pies on St Stephen's Day (better known now as Boxing Day, 26th December) and give some to needier neighbours who could not afford to make their own. Those who were not lucky recipients of Goose Pies could always make do with this cheaper alternative dish, which was not actually made from goose but from ox liver.

>   450g/1 lb ox liver
>   Seasoned flour
>   A small amount of oil or fat for frying
>   3 onions, sliced
>   1 tablespoonful chopped sage
>   300ml/ ½ pint stock
>   450g/1 lb potatoes
>   A small knob of butter

Pre-heat the oven to 180°C/350°F/Gas Mark 4.

Slice the liver into thin strips and coat them in the seasoned flour. Fry the sliced onions in the oil or fat until they are soft, then add the liver and fry lightly for 2 minutes. Put the liver and onions into an ovenproof dish, sprinkle over the chopped sage, and then pour over the stock. Peel the potatoes and cut them into thin slices. Arrange the potato slices on top of the liver and onions. Cover the dish with a lid or foil, and bake in the pre-heated oven for 1 hour. Remove the lid or foil for the last 20 minutes of the cooking time, and brush the potatoes with melted butter to make them brown and crisp at the edges.

— · —

RECIPE

— · —

Wakefield Rabbit

4 rabbit joints

Seasoned flour

1 egg, beaten

50g/2oz dried breadcrumbs

1 level teaspoonful mixed dried herbs - thyme,
 marjoram and parsley

A pinch of cayenne pepper, to taste

Salt

25g/1oz butter

Pre-heat the oven to 180°C/350°F/Gas Mark 4.

Toss the rabbit joints in the seasoned flour, coating all sides. Mix the
breadcrumbs with the herbs, salt and pepper and cayenne pepper.
Dip each rabbit joint in the beaten egg, and then coat it with the
herby breadcrumb mixture.

Put the rabbit joints in a roasting tin, and dot the top of each joint
with small pieces of butter. Roast the joints in the pre-heated oven for
about 1½ hours, or until the joints have a crispy finish.

— · —

Hawes, Haymaking 1924 75754

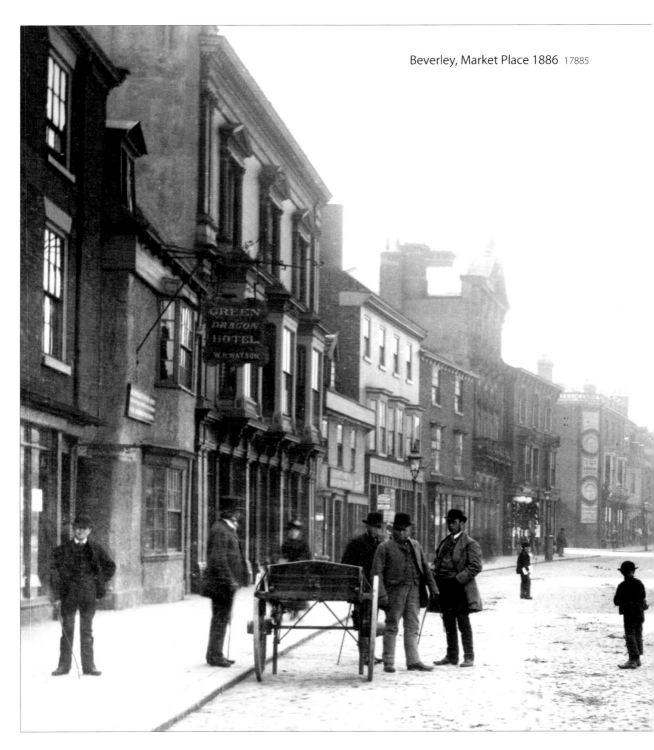

Beverley, Market Place 1886 17885

CHEESE, EGG AND SUPPER DISHES

Dock Pudding

The Calder Valley of Yorkshire is famous for its Dock Pudding, which is fried in bacon fat and eaten for breakfast or supper. The plant used is not the common dock, however, but bistort, or sweet dock, which is similar to spinach. It grows in the early spring, and so in former years it was a useful food plant as it provided some fresh greens during the time of the year known as the 'hungry gap', when winter food stores were running out and not much else was yet ready to harvest. A traditional Dock Pudding also contained nettles, wild garlic and oatmeal. The tradition is remembered in the World Dock Pudding Championships which are held every April or May in Mytholmroyd in the Calder Valley.

Doncaster, A Tram in Station Road 1903 49854x

RECIPE

—·—

Bacon and Egg Pie

450g/1 lb shortcrust pastry
2 tablespoonfuls cooking oil
6 rashers of bacon
1 small onion, finely chopped
4 eggs
1 tablespoonful chopped fresh parsley (optional)
Salt
Black pepper
Beaten egg or milk to glaze pastry lid

Grease a deep 20cm (8inch) flan tin. Roll out two thirds of the pastry on a lightly floured surface, and use it to line the tin, making sure that the pastry comes right up to the top of the sides. Cover the tin and chill in the fridge with the remaining pastry whilst the filling is prepared.

Pre-heat the oven to 200°C/400°F/Gas Mark 6.

Remove the rind from the bacon rashers, and cut each rasher into several pieces. Heat the oil in a saucepan, add the bacon pieces and cook until the bacon fat is running, then add the onion. Cook gently until the onion is softened, then remove the mixture from the pan and drain on kitchen paper, and leave to cool for a few minutes.

Spread half the bacon and onion mixture evenly over the base of the pastry case. Carefully break the eggs whole over the filling, spacing them apart so that there is one in each quarter of the pie. Tilt the tin a little to make the egg whites flow evenly across the filling and run together. Add seasoning over the eggs, using plenty of black pepper but adjusting the salt to taste, depending on how salty the bacon is, and sprinkle over the fresh chopped parsley, if used. Spread the remaining half of the bacon and onion mixture over the eggs.

Roll out the remaining pastry on a floured surface to a size to cover the flan tin, dampen the edges and place over the dish. Roll over the top with the rolling pin to seal the edges, and trim off the excess pastry. Make hole in the centre of the lid with a sharp knife to allow the steam to escape, and brush the lid with beaten egg or milk, to glaze the pastry.

Bake the pie in the pre-heated oven for 10 minutes, then reduce the heat to 180°C/350°F/Gas Mark 4 and continue to bake for another 20 minutes, until the pastry is crisp and golden brown.

—·—

Carlton, The Post Office 1926   79051x

RECIPE

—·—

Panacalty

There are many versions of Panacalty, which can either be cooked in the oven or simmered in a saucepan on the top of the stove. This dish can also be made using pork sausages or liver, and a version using tinned corned beef is also popular. Panacalty is traditionally accompanied with thick slices of good bread, buttered or not, according to preference.

450g/1 lb bacon

4 potatoes

1 large onion

Salt and pepper

600ml/1 pint stock

Peel the potatoes and cut them into slices. Peel the onion and slice it into rings. Put a small amount of stock in the bottom of a large heavy saucepan. Place a layer of potatoes into the pan, then cover with a layer of bacon and then onion, seasoning each layer. Repeat the layers, until all the ingredients have been used. Add the stock, cover with the saucepan lid and bring to the boil, then turn down the heat and leave to simmer gently for 25-30 minutes until the potatoes are cooked and tender.

Alternatively, place the layers into a large ovenproof dish, cover with the lid and cook in a pre-heated oven (180°C/350°F/Gas Mark 4) for 30-40 minutes.

—·—

Knaresborough stands above the River Nidd on a sandstone cliff. It is said that Mother Shipton was born in a cave in the cliff here in the 15th century, and the Mother Shipton Inn, formerly a farmhouse, stands in front of that cave. Mother Shipton was renowned as a prophetess; she wrote her prophecies in verse, and among other things foretold Sir Walter Raleigh's discovery of tobacco and potatoes in America:

'From whence he shall bring
A herb and a root
That all men shall suit,
And please both the ploughman and the king'.

Knaresborough, The Mother Shipton Inn 1914 67264

RECITE

—·—

Yorkshire Rarebit

This is a good way of using up some leftover pieces of cooked ham. It can also be served with a fried egg on top, when it is known as Buck Rarebit.

> 25g/1oz butter
> 1 level tablespoonful plain flour
> 5 tablespoonfuls of milk
> 175g/6oz Wensleydale cheese, grated
> 50g/2oz cooked ham, cut into small pieces
> 1 teaspoonful of made mustard
> A dash of Worcestershire Sauce
> Salt and pepper
> Slices of bread for toasting
> Butter

Melt the butter in a saucepan, and stir in the flour. Cook gently for a few minutes, then add the milk, a very little at a time, stirring the mixture continuously until it thickens.

Add the cheese, ham, mustard and Worcestershire Sauce. Season with salt and pepper to taste.

Toast and butter slices of bread. Spread the mixture onto the toasted slices and place under a hot grill. Grill until they are golden brown and bubbling.

—·—

A Taste of YORKSHIRE

Askrigg, Women outside the Post Office 1911 63469x

Ingleton, The Bus 1929 82711v

RECIPE

Yorkshire Old Wives' Sod

This is a very old traditional recipe making use of oatcakes, which were a staple food in Yorkshire in the past. It results in a thick savoury custard, which can be eaten as a supper dish.

5 large eggs
450ml/ ¾ pint milk
Salt and pepper to taste
25g/1oz butter
2 thin oat cakes, lightly toasted, then buttered and broken into pieces

Pre-heat the oven to 160°C/325°F/Gas Mark 3.

Break the eggs into a mixing bowl and beat well. Stir in the milk, salt and pepper and mix together thoroughly. Grease an oven-proof dish and pour in the mixture. Sprinkle the broken oat cakes into the mixture, and dot the top with small pieces of butter.

Bake in the pre-heated oven for about 20 minutes.

PUDDINGS, PIES AND DESSERTS

Scarborough, South Bay c1873 6560

RECIPE

—·—

Summer Pudding

Summer Pudding was a popular dessert with visitors to hydropathic establishments in spa towns such as Scarborough and Harrogate because it was lighter than pastry-based puddings, which were thought to be heavy and indigestible. For this reason it was sometimes known as Hydropathic Pudding.

> 10 slices of crustless white bread – use bread from a proper loaf, not a sliced and wrapped one, for best results
>
> 3 tablespoonfuls of milk
>
> 750g/1½ lbs soft fruit – use a variety of such fruits as raspberries, cherries, redcurrants, blackcurrants, white currants, loganberries or (sparingly) strawberries
>
> 115g/4oz caster sugar

Reserve a few pieces of fresh fruit to decorate.

Lightly butter a pudding basin of 1 litre (1¾ pint) capacity. Moisten the bread with milk. Hull, stone or top and tail the fruit as necessary. Cook it all very gently in a saucepan in the sugar for 4-5 minutes until the sugar melts and the juices run. Spoon off a few spoonfuls of the juice as it cools and reserve. Line the sides and bottom of the pudding basin with the bread slices, cutting them to fit where necessary and checking that there are no spaces. Reserve enough bread slices for a lid. Pour in the fruit, which should come almost to the top, and cover closely with the remaining bread. Put a small plate over the top (it should just fit inside the rim of the basin), and weight it with something heavy. Leave to press overnight in the fridge.

To serve, remove the weight and the plate. Place a deep serving dish over the top of the pudding basin and reverse quickly so that the pudding comes out easily in one piece. Pour the remaining juices slowly all over the pudding, especially over the places where the juice has not seeped through the bread slices thoroughly. Keep cold until ready to serve, then decorate with a few pieces of fruit and serve with cream.

—·—

Harrogate, James Street 1914 67283

York, The Cavalry Barracks, Sword Practice 1886 18716x

RECIPE

—·—

Gooseberry and Elderflower Cream

The town of Egton Bridge on the North Yorkshire Moors is still known for its annual gooseberry show, held in August, where gardeners compete to see who has grown the largest or tastiest gooseberries.

500g/1½ lbs gooseberries
30ml/2 tablespoonfuls elderflower cordial
300ml/10 fl oz double cream
115g/4oz icing sugar

Place the gooseberries in a heavy saucepan, cover and cook over a low heat, shaking the pan occasionally until they are tender. Tip the gooseberries into a bowl, crush them with a heavy wooden spoon or potato masher, then leave them to cool completely. (The gooseberries can be sieved or pureed if a finer consistency is preferred.) Beat the cream until soft peaks form, then gently fold in half the crushed gooseberries. Sweeten with icing sugar to taste, and fold in the elderflower cordial. Sweeten the remaining gooseberries with icing sugar to taste. Put a layer of the cream mixture in four dessert dishes or tall glasses, and then a layer of crushed gooseberries, then cover and chill for at least one hour before serving.

—·—

RECITE

— · —

West Riding Pudding

175g/6oz shortcrust pastry
2 tablespoonfuls of raspberry jam
115g/4oz butter
115g/4oz caster sugar
2 eggs, beaten
115g/4oz self-raising flour
25g/1oz ground almonds
Grated zest of half a lemon

Pre-heat the oven to 180°C/350°F/Gas Mark 4.

Roll out the pastry on a lightly floured surface, and use it to line a greased 20cm (8 inch) pie tin. Spread the base of the tart with raspberry jam.

Cream the butter and sugar together in a bowl until the mixture is light and fluffy. Beat in the eggs a little at a time, adding a little flour if necessary to prevent curdling. Sift the flour into the mixture, then add the ground almonds and grated lemon zest, and gently fold it all in. Turn the mixture into the pie tin and spread it over the jam. Bake in the pre-heated oven for 25-30 minutes, until the filling is well risen and firm and the pastry is golden and crisp.

— · —

Halifax, Town Hall 1900 H9001

RECIPE

—— · ——

Yorkshire Apple and Honey Pudding

115g/4oz butter or margarine

115g/4oz caster sugar

115g/4oz plain flour

2 eggs, beaten

50g/2oz soft brown sugar

2 cooking apples

115g/4oz runny honey

A pinch of grated nutmeg

A pinch of salt

Cream the butter and sugar until it is fluffy, then beat in the eggs a little at a time, adding a small amount of flour if necessary to prevent the mixture from curdling. Sift the flour and a pinch of salt into the bowl, and gently fold in until it is all mixed in. Grease a pudding basin and sprinkle the brown sugar over the bottom and around the sides of the dish. Peel, core and slice the apples and put them in the bottom of the basin, then sprinkle the grated nutmeg and dribble the honey over the apple slices. Pour the creamed mixture into the basin and gently spread the surface to cover the apple.

Cover the basin with its lid or a piece of pleated greaseproof paper, tied down securely. Half fill a large saucepan with water, bring to the boil and place the pudding basin inside the saucepan. Replace the lid and steam for 1½ - 2 hours. Check the pan regularly and replenish with more boiling water when necessary, making sure that it does not boil dry.

When the pudding is cooked, turn out from the basin into a serving dish and serve with cream or custard, and a little warmed honey if liked.

This can be cooked in a pressure cooker if preferred, for 45 minutes. It can also be cooked in a microwave oven: use a microwave-safe bowl, and cook on high for 4-5 minutes. To make sure that it is cooked all the way through, wait 2 minutes, then plunge a thin blade into the centre of the pudding. If it has some batter sticking to it, put the pudding back in the oven and microwave for 1 minute longer.

—— · ——

Saltaire, The Mill and the Cricket Pitch 1888 21024

RECIPE

— . —

Ginger Sponge Pudding

At the bottom of Whitefriargate in the centre of Hull Old Town is one of the most intriguingly-named streets in England – Land of Green Ginger. It was formerly known as Old Beverley Street. There are several theories as to how the street got this name, but the explanation preferred by John Markwell in 'Street Names of Hull' is that this was the part of town where green, or unripe, ginger used to be stored.

This sponge pudding also makes a delicious soft gingerbread when eaten cold.

> 175g/6oz self-raising flour
> 75g/3oz caster sugar
> 1 heaped teaspoonful ground ginger
> 50ml/2fl oz milk
> 75g/3oz margarine
> 1 good tablespoonful of golden syrup
> 1 teaspoonful bicarbonate of soda
> A little extra golden syrup to finish

Pre-heat the oven to 160°C/325°F/Gas Mark 3.

Mix the flour, sugar and ginger together. Put the milk, margarine and syrup into a large saucepan, and bring to the boil. Sir well, until the margarine and syrup have melted. Remove the pan from the heat and stir in the bicarbonate of soda.

Add the flour, sugar and ginger to the milk and syrup mixture, and mix it all well together. Turn the mixture into a well-greased cake tin 20cm (8inch) square, and bake just above the centre of the pre-heated oven for 30 minutes.

Just before serving, warm a little extra golden syrup in a saucepan and pour over the pudding. Serve hot, with custard or cream.

— . —

Local words and phrases from the Hull area

'A penny all off' - a short back and sides, as in a hair cut.

'Booling' - pushing a pram or bike.

'Flag edge' - the kerb of a pavement.

'Gassunder' - a chamberpot; the term comes from the fact that it 'goes under' the bed.

'I'm mafted' - I'm really hot, also 'mafting', as in 'It's mafting' - The weather's really hot.

'Spanish' - liquorice.

'Worrawolly' - a simpleton, fool.

'Dowly' - miserable, damp or dreary weather.

'Taffled' - tangled.

'Laid out like a shilling dinner' - Sprawled, as in all over the sofa.

Hull, Whitefriargate 1903 49817

RECITE

—·—

Bilberry Pie

Bilberries can be found on the Yorkshire moors throughout late summer. They are also known as blueberries or blaeberries. They grow on small bushes close to the ground and are hard work to pick, but are well worth the effort.

450g/1 lb bilberries
2 cooking apples
225g/8oz sugar
1 egg, beaten
350g/12oz sweet shortcrust or puff pastry, whichever is preferred

Remove the cores from the apples with an apple corer, but do not peel them. Stand the apples in an ovenproof dish, add 2 tablespoonfuls of water to the dish and bake in the preheated oven for 40-45 minutes, until the apples are tender. When cooked, scrape out the pulp from the apples and mix it with the bilberries and the sugar.

Pre-heat the oven to 200°C/400°F/Gas Mark 6.

Roll out half the pastry on a lightly floured board and use it to line a greased 20cm (8 inch) pie tin. Turn out the fruit mixture into the pie tin. Roll out the remaining pastry to make a lid and place it over the pie, and trim and seal the edges.

Brush the lid of the pie with beaten egg white and sprinkle with sugar. Place in the pre-heated oven and bake for ten minutes, then reduce the heat to 180°/350°C/Gas Mark 4 and cook for a further 30 minutes until the pastry is golden brown and crisp.

—·—

Slices of Wensleydale cheese are a favourite addition to the filling of an apple pie in Yorkshire.

'An apple pie without Wensleydale cheese
Is like a kiss without a squeeze.'

Filey, Primrose Valley c1935 F23099

RECIPE

—.—

Yorkshire Curd Tart

The distinguishing and traditional characteristic of Yorkshire Curd Tart is allspice (or 'clove pepper' as it was also known) but this may not be to modern tastes, so mixed spice can be substituted for the ground allspice if preferred.

For the pastry:
115g/4oz butter, diced
225g/8oz plain flour
1 egg yolk

For the filling:
A large pinch of ground allspice, or mixed spice if preferred
90g/3½ oz sugar
3 eggs, beaten
Grated rind and juice of 1 lemon
40g/1½ oz melted butter
450g/1 lb curd cheese, or cottage cheese if curd cheese is hard to find
75g/3oz raisins or sultanas

Pre-heat the oven to 190°C/375°F/Gas Mark 5.

To make the pastry: rub the butter into the flour until the mixture resembles fine breadcrumbs. Stir the egg yolk into the flour mixture with a little water to bind the dough together. Turn the dough on to a lightly floured surface, knead lightly and form into a ball. Roll out the pastry thinly and use to line a 20cm (8 inch) fluted loose-bottomed flan tin. Chill for 15 minutes.

To make the filling: mix the ground allspice or mixed spice with the sugar, then stir in the eggs, lemon rind and juice, melted butter, curd or cottage cheese and dried fruit. Pour the filling into the chilled pastry case, then bake in the pre-heated oven for about 40 minutes until the pastry is cooked and the filling is lightly set and golden brown. Serve still slightly warm, cut into wedges with cream.

—.—

Knaresborough, Market Day 1921 71687

TEATIME AND BAKING

~·~

RECIPE

~·~

Yorkshire Bun Loaf

275g/10oz self-raising flour
115g/4oz margarine
75g/3oz caster sugar
2 eggs, beaten
2 teaspoonfuls marmalade
75g/3oz sultanas
75g/3oz currants
A little milk

Pre-heat the oven to 190°C/375°F/Gas Mark 5.

Sift the flour into a bowl. Rub in the margarine, then stir in the sugar, eggs, marmalade, sultanas and currants. Bind to a medium stiff mixture with milk, then turn into a greased 500g/1 lb loaf tin. Sprinkle the top with caster sugar and bake in the pre-heated oven for 1 hour.

~·~

RECEIPE

—·—

Parkin

The black treacle gives this the true dark parkin colour.

300ml/ ½ pint milk
225g/8oz golden syrup
225g/8oz black treacle
115g/4oz butter or margarine
50g/2oz dark brown sugar
450g/1 lb plain flour
Half a teaspoonful of bicarbonate of soda
1½ teaspoonfuls of ground ginger
350g/12oz medium oatmeal
1 egg, beaten

Pre-heat the oven to 180°C/350°F/Gas Mark 4.

Put the milk, syrup, treacle, butter or margarine and sugar into a saucepan and heat gently, stirring all the time, until the mixture has melted and is smooth. Take care not to let the mixture boil. When it has mixed together, take it off the heat and leave to cool for a few minutes.

Put the flour, bicarbonate of soda, ginger and oatmeal into a large bowl and mix together. Make a well in the centre, pour in the beaten egg, then gradually pour in the milk and syrup mixture, stirring all the time, until it has formed a smooth batter.

Grease a 20cm (8 inch) square cake tin, and line the bottom with greaseproof paper. Pour the batter into the tin. Bake in the pre-heated oven for about 45 minutes, until the surface of the parkin is firm to the touch.

Allow the parkin to cool in the tin for a few minutes, then turn out on to a wire rack to cool completely. Cut into pieces when cool, and store in an airtight tin, preferably for 3 days, before eating.

—·—

RECIPE

—·—

Yorkshire Cheesecake Tarts

For the pastry:
115g/4oz butter or margarine
225g/8oz plain flour
1 tablespoonful caster sugar
Pinch of salt
1 egg yolk
1-2 tablespoons cold water

For the filling:
225g/8oz fresh curd or cottage
   cheese, sieved
50g/2oz caster sugar
1 teaspoonful grated lemon rind
2 eggs, separated
2 tablespoonfuls currants or
   sultanas
1 tablespoonful melted butter
Pinch of nutmeg

Make the pastry by rubbing the fat into the flour, adding the sugar, salt and egg yolk, and mixing well. Finally add the cold water to make a firm dough. Turn out on to a floured surface and knead well, then roll into a ball and chill for at least 30 minutes.

Pre-heat the oven to 220°C/425°F/Gas Mark 7.

Mix together all the remaining ingredients except the egg whites. Roll out the pastry. Line 12 greased deep patty tins with the pastry, and lightly prick over the bottoms with a fork.

Beat the egg whites until stiff, and lightly fold into the cheese mixture. Divide the mixture between the patty tin cases, and cook in the pre-heated oven for 10 minutes, then reduce the oven temperature to 180°C/350°F/Gas Mark 4, and continue cooking for a further 20-25 minutes or until the cheese mixture is set and golden.

—·—

Local words and phrases from the Sheffield area

'Well, I'll go the foot of our stairs!' - I'm really surprised.

'Clemmed' - very cold, frozen through.

'Nesh' - feeling the cold, as in 'I'm a bit nesh'.

'Laykin' - skiving off school or work.

'Mardy' - peevish, querulous, miserable, moody, sulking.

'Snicket' - a pathway between hedges, fences etc.

'I'm stood 'ere like Clem Alice!' - I'm standing here waiting, looking like a complete idiot!

Sheffield, The Canal Basin 1870 S108301

RECIPE

—.—

Yorkshire Fat Rascals

These teacakes with a rich crust are particularly associated with the Cleveland area of Yorkshire. They are sort of cross between scones and rock cakes.

450g/1 lb self-raising flour

115g/4oz lard

115g/4oz butter

50g/2oz light soft brown sugar

Pinch of salt

Grated zest of 1 lemon and 1 orange

Half a teaspoonful of cinnamon

115g/4oz currants

A small quantity of milk and water mixed

Pre-heat the oven to 180°C/350°F/Gas Mark 4.

Rub the butter into the flour. Add the sugar, salt, lemon and orange zest, cinnamon and currants and mix to a firm dough with a little mixed water and milk. Roll out to about 1cm (½ inch) thick, and cut into 6cm (2½ inch) rounds. Dust with a little caster sugar and bake in the pre-heated oven for about 20 minutes.

—.—

In many parts of Yorkshire it was traditional to make a 'Pepper Cake' at Christmas, which was flavoured with black treacle and allspice, or clove pepper as it was known locally. Pepper Cake was served with a piece of cheese to visitors such as carol singers, and was the subject of a seasonal rhyme sung by children:

'A little bit of pepper cake,
A little bit of cheese,
A little drink of water,
And a penny, if you please!'

Grassington, Children in the Square 1926 79060x

Redcar, The Sands 1886 18133

RECIPE

~·~

Moggy

175g/6oz plain flour

Half a teaspoonful of baking powder

A small pinch of salt

75g/3oz margarine

50g/2oz golden syrup

50g/2oz sugar

A small amount of milk for mixing

Pre-heat the oven to 180°C/350°F/Gas Mark 4.

Mix the flour, baking powder and salt in a mixing bowl. Cut the margarine into small pieces and rub into the flour, until the mixture resembles fine breadcrumbs. Add the sugar and golden syrup and mix in. Add a small amount of milk, just enough to form a stiff dough, and knead the dough for a few minutes to mix it all together well.

Turn the dough out onto a lightly floured surface and roll it out to about 3cm (1½ inches) thick. Place the dough on a greased baking sheet and bake in the pre-heated oven for about 30 minutes, until it is nicely browned. Cut into pieces and eat whilst it is still warm, spread with butter.

~·~

Settle, Market Day 1921 71339

RECIPE

— · —

Wilfra Tarts

These little tarts were traditionally made in Ripon during Wilfra Week in August, a festival commemorating St Wilfrid, the patron saint of Ripon Cathedral.

225g/8oz shortcrust pastry
300ml/ ½ pint of milk
25g/1oz fresh white breadcrumbs
115g/4oz butter
50g/2oz ground almonds
3 eggs, beaten
25g/1oz caster sugar
Grated zest of 1 lemon

Pre-heat the oven to 180°C/350°F/Gas Mark 4.

Bring the milk to the boil in a saucepan, and pour it over the breadcrumbs in a mixing bowl. Stir, and leave for 10 minutes for the breadcrumbs to absorb the milk.

Grease a tray of patty tins. Roll out the pastry on a lightly floured surface, and use it to line the patty tins.

Cut the butter into small pieces and add to the milk and breadcrumbs. Stir in until the butter has melted. Add the ground almonds, sugar and grated lemon zest. Beat in the eggs, a little at a time. Fill the pastry cases in the patty tins with the mixture, and bake in the pre-heated oven until the filling is risen and set.

— · —

Ripon, The Cathedral c1955
R38012

Skipton, High Street 1900 45757

RECIPE

—·—

Cable Cakes

50g/2oz margarine
25g/1oz caster sugar
225g/8oz plain flour
1 teaspoonful baking powder
225g/8oz mincemeat (about two thirds of a jar)
1 egg, beaten
A small amount of milk for mixing

Pre-heat the oven to 230°C/450°F/Gas Mark 8.

Cream the margarine and sugar together until the mixture is light and fluffy. Sift the flour and baking powder together and add to the mixture, and then mix in the mincemeat. Add the beaten egg and enough milk to form a stiff dough, and mix well together.

Spoon the mixture into paper cases, place on a tray and bake in the pre-heated oven for about 15 minutes, until the cakes are risen and lightly browned, and firm but springy to the touch.

—·—

Middlesbrough, Corporation Road
1901 47979

Selby, The Cross and Gowthorpe 1903 49865

RECIPE

~ . ~

Apple Fritters

Apple fritters used to be a traditional treat for Ash Wednesday.

225g/8oz flour
3 eggs
300ml/ ½ pint of milk
225g/8oz currants
4 cooking apples
Lard or oil for frying
Caster or icing sugar for dredging.

Sift the flour into a large mixing bowl and make a well in the centre. Break the eggs into the well, and beat them into the flour, drawing the flour in from the sides, until it has all mixed together thoroughly into a smooth paste. Gradually add the milk, a little at a time, beating continually to make a batter.

Pore and core the apples and chop them into small pieces. Mix the apple pieces and the currants into the batter.

Heat the lard or oil in a large pan. Drop in spoonfuls of the batter and fry the fritters until they are crisp and golden. Drain and dry on absorbent kitchen paper, then dredge with sugar and eat whilst still hot.

~ . ~

Local words and phrases from the Leeds area

An inhabitant of Leeds is traditionally known as a **'Loiner'**, a term derived from the word 'Loin' for a roll of cloth, and thus a reference to Leeds as a centre of the cloth trade.

'Ah'm sad flayed' - I'm a bit stupid.

'Get agate then' - get on with it.

'Moudiwarp' - a mole.

'Fuzzock' - a donkey.

'Leit green' - crafty, cunning.

Leeds, The Post Office and Revenue Office 1897 39088

RECITPE

—.—

Treacle Toffee

Bonfire Night on 5th November commemorates the foiled Gunpowder Plot of 1605 to blow up James I and his parliament in London with 36 barrels of gunpowder. Guy Fawkes, who was recruited by the Gunpowder Plotters because of his expertise with gunpowder gained during his military career, was caught in the cellars of the House of Lords, apparently about to set fire to the fuse which would set off the explosion. Treacle Toffee is traditionally eaten in Yorkshire on Bonfire Night, and is particularly appropriate for York as Guy Fawkes himself was born in the city in 1570. In some parts of Yorkshire the toffee is twisted into long lengths and is known as Tom Trot Toffee.

> 450g/1 lb soft brown sugar
> 5 tablespoonfuls of water
> 2 teaspoonfuls of vinegar
> 25g/1oz butter
> 150ml/ ¼ pint black treacle

Put the sugar into a saucepan with the water and vinegar and when dissolved add the butter and the treacle. Heat gently until the butter and treacle melt. Raise the heat and boil for 12-15 minutes. The temperature can be checked with a sugar thermometer, and should reach around 140°C or 280°F.

Pour the treacle into a greased or oiled tin and leave until partially set. Score the toffee with a knife into bars or squares, and when cold break up and store in an airtight tin.

—.—

Richmond, The Castle Keep 1908 59493

York, Goodramgate 1892 30631

Ilkley, The Grove 1911 63556

Pontefract Cakes

The Crusaders of the 12th century probably introduced the liquorice plant to Pontefract, and from that grew a hugely important industry; it still flourishes today, but the liquorice roots are no longer grown locally. The disc-shaped sweets flavoured with liquorice known as Pontefract Cakes (or 'Pomfret' or 'Pomfrey' Cakes) are still made in the town, and an annual liquorice festival is held there, where liquorice flavoured cheese, ice cream and beer can be sampled. Liquorice is known as 'Spanish' in some parts of Yorkshire.

INDEX OF PHOTOGRAPHS

INDEX OF RECIPES

FREE PRINT OF YOUR CHOICE

Mounted Print
Overall size 14 x 11 inches (355 x 280mm)

Choose any Frith photograph in this book.
Simply complete the Voucher opposite and return it with your remittance for £3.50 (to cover postage and handling) and we will print the photograph of your choice in SEPIA (size 11 x 8 inches) and supply it in a cream mount with a burgundy rule line (overall size 14 x 11 inches).
Please note: aerial photographs and photographs with a reference number starting with a "Z" are not Frith photographs and cannot be supplied under this offer. Offer valid for delivery to one UK address only.

PLUS: Order additional Mounted Prints at HALF PRICE - £9.50 each (normally £19.00)
If you would like to order more Frith prints from this book, possibly as gifts for friends and family, you can buy them at half price (with no additional postage and handling costs).

PLUS: Have your Mounted Prints framed
For an extra £18.00 per print you can have your mounted print(s) framed in an elegant polished wood and gilt moulding, overall size 16 x 13 inches (no additional postage and handling required).

IMPORTANT!

These special prices are only available if you use this form to order. You must use the ORIGINAL VOUCHER on this page (no copies permitted). We can only despatch to one UK address. This offer cannot be combined with any other offer.

Send completed Voucher form to:
The Francis Frith Collection, Frith's Barn, Teffont, Salisbury, Wiltshire SP3 5QP

CHOOSE A PHOTOGRAPH FROM THIS BOOK

Voucher for **FREE** and Reduced Price Frith Prints

Please do not photocopy this voucher. Only the original is valid, so please fill it in, cut it out and return it to us with your order.

Picture ref no	Page no	Qty	Mounted @ £9.50	Framed + £18.00	Total Cost £
		1	Free of charge*	£	£
			£9.50	£	£
			£9.50	£	£
			£9.50	£	£
			£9.50	£	£
			£9.50	£	£

Please allow 28 days for delivery. Offer available to one UK address only

* Post & handling		£3.50
Total Order Cost		£

Title of this book . . . .
I enclose a cheque/postal order for £ . . . .
made payable to 'The Francis Frith Collection'

OR please debit my Mastercard / Visa / Maestro card, details below

Card Number

Issue No (Maestro only)   Valid from (Maestro)

Expires   Signature

Name Mr/Mrs/Ms . . . .
Address . . . .
. . . .
. . . .
. . . . Postcode . . . .
Daytime Tel No . . . .
Email . . . .

978-1-84589-422-1   Valid to 31/12/11

Can you help us with information about any of the Frith photographs in this book?

We are gradually compiling an historical record for each of the photographs in the Frith archive. It is always fascinating to find out the names of the people shown in the pictures, as well as insights into the shops, buildings and other features depicted.

If you recognize anyone in the photographs in this book, or if you have information not already included in the author's caption, do let us know. We would love to hear from you, and will try to publish it in future books or articles.

An Invitation from The Francis Frith Collection to Share Your Memories

The 'Share Your Memories' feature of our website allows members of the public to add personal memories relating to the places featured in our photographs, or comment on others already added. Seeing a place from your past can rekindle forgotten or long held memories. Why not visit the website, find photographs of places you know well and add YOUR story for others to read and enjoy? We would love to hear from you!

www.francisfrith.com/memories

Our production team

Frith books are produced by a small dedicated team at offices in the converted Grade II listed 18th-century barn at Teffont near Salisbury, illustrated above. Most have worked with the Frith Collection for many years. All have in common one quality: they have a passion for the Frith Collection.

Frith Books and Gifts

We have a wide range of books and gifts available on our website utilising our photographic archive, many of which can be individually personalised.

www.francisfrith.com